# Ricky & the Moose
## The Story of the MooseMan

**Text and photos by Rick Libbey**
**Illustrations by Donna Libbey**

AuthorHouse™
1663 Liberty Drive, Suite 200
Bloomington, IN 47403
www.authorhouse.com
Phone: 1-800-839-8640

© 2008 Rick Libbey. All rights reserved.

No part of this book may be reproduced, stored in a retrieval system, or transmitted by any means without the written permission of the author.

First published by AuthorHouse 6/30/2008

ISBN: 978-1-4343-9209-1 (sc)

Printed in the United States of America
Bloomington, Indiana

This book is printed on acid-free paper.

# To our grandchildren
# Emma, Annabella, Alexis, Haili, and Bryce

A special thank you from the author

My Mom Priscilla and my Dad Howard for giving me their goodness and strong character.

My wife and soul-mate Donna for her drawings in this book but even more for her support and encouragement as I follow my true calling with the moose and the wilderness.

My four step-children Bobby, Matt, Valerie, and Sherry who also encouraged me to pursue my dream.

My sister Claudia who gave me endless love as a child.

Mary Gutgsell, my dear friend....thanks for assistance in this book and in life as well.

Chris Flagg, my long time friend and big influence on my love for nature.

Andy Atsma, many trips to the wilderness with this man, and more to come.

Marcy and Amy at Artisan's, whose support and friendship are dear to me.

Everyone at Flash Photo, the small town photo store that has been wonderful in helping me get to where I indeed will go. A special thanks to Angela and Robert for their expertise and enthusiasm.

And lastly........To all the MOOSE. When I am out there in the woods with them, I feel full contentment within myself.

Ricky lived on a farm in the woods. There was a pond out behind the barn. Young Ricky loved that pond and all the animals that lived there. Especially the MOOSE!

One summer day on the farm there was a birthday party for Ricky. His favorite present that day was a camera he got from his Dad. Ricky dreamed of being a professional nature photographer someday......BUT......

He had a lot to learn. He made too much noise and scared the moose away.

When he chased them trying to get a good picture, the moose went even faster; crashing off into the woods.

He asked his Dad what was wrong.

"You have to be very, very quiet in the woods," his Dad said. "You have to go very slow out there."

As Ricky grew older he learned to sit quietly and he blended into the woods with camouflage clothing. One day he decided to go out in his kayak.

As the years went by Ricky spent more time in the wilderness. By now he had learned not only to be quiet but also to stay downwind of the moose.

Ricky learned to respect the moose and their environment. The moose began to trust him. Some were curious and even approached him peacefully.

Bill The Bull

Big Boy

Ricky observed many of the same moose year after year and even gave them names.

Pot Belly

and her baby, Sweet Pea

Ricky became a famous nature photographer just like he dreamed.

A Gal

And Ricky knows he owes it all to the MOOSE.

Printed in the United States
117948LV00003B